THE FINAL FOUR

The PURSUIT of COLLEGE BASKETBALL GLORY

Matt Doeden

M MILLBROOK PRESS · MINNEAPOLIS

Millbrook Press
A division of Lerner Publishing Group, Inc.
241 First Avenue North
Minneapolis, MN 55401 USA

For reading levels and more information, look up this title at www.lernerbooks.com.

Library of Congress Cataloging-in-Publication Data

Doeden, Matt.
    The Final Four : the pursuit of college basketball glory / by Matt Doeden.
       pages cm. — (Spectacular sports)
    Includes bibliographical references and index.
    Audience: Age: 10–18.
    Audience: Grade: 9 to 12.
    ISBN 978-1-4677-8780-2 (lb : alk. paper) — ISBN 978-1-4677-9730-6 (eb pdf)
    1. NCAA Basketball Tournament—History—Juvenile literature. I. Title.
GV885.49.N37D64 2016
796.323'63–dc23   2015025429

Manufactured in the United States of America
1 – CG – 12/31/15

CONTENTS

INTRODUCTION
March Madness

The clock ticks down the seconds . . . 5 . . . 4 . . . The roar of the crowd is deafening. A player drives toward the basket, stops, steps back . . . 3 . . . 2 . . . 1 . . .The shot goes up. Camera flashes fill the arena. The clock strikes 0 as the ball banks off the backboard and drops toward the rim.

Few sporting events can match the pure excitement of the Final Four. After a tough regular season and weeks of battling through the National Collegiate Athletic Association (NCAA) Division 1 Men's Basketball Championship tournament, four teams gather to try to stake their claims as the best in the land. For more than three-quarters of a century, the Final Four has given fans thrills, chills, and more than a share of heartbreak. It's college basketball's biggest stage, and only one team can survive.

Opposite page: The Duke Blue Devils and the Wisconsin Badgers battle in the 2015 NCAA title game.

1

FROM THE BASEMENT TO THE BIG TIME

A History of the College Basketball Championship

There were no cameras, no packed seats, and no food vendors at Hamline University in St. Paul, Minnesota, on February 9, 1895. No fanfare of any kind. No one could have known it at the time, but in the basement of the university's science building, history was being made.

It wasn't the splitting of the atom, the discovery of genetics, or the theory of relativity that made history that day in Science Hall. It was a basketball game. Basketball was a new sport, invented by physical education teacher James Naismith less than four years earlier. Hamline's athletic director, Ray Kaighn, had played on Naismith's first basketball team. Kaighn brought the sport to Minnesota. When he invited players from the nearby School of Agriculture (part of the present-day University of Minnesota) to campus for a friendly game, the first intercollegiate basketball game was on.

Opposite page: James Naismith *(center, right)* invented basketball in 1891.

There should be little surprise that a game played in the basement of a science building didn't look much like the modern sport. The teams played with nine players on each side and shot at peach baskets hung on the walls. Even the final score—a 9–3 victory for the visiting team—would seem much too low to modern fans. Yet a college tradition was born that day. It wouldn't take long before college basketball moved out of the basement and into the big time.

EVOLVING GAME

Basketball rapidly grew in popularity. Less than a year after that first college game in Minnesota, the University of Iowa invited players from the University of Chicago for a contest. This game looked a bit more like the sport fans love today. It featured five players on each side, and the scores actually reached double digits (a 15–12 victory for Chicago).

Over the decades, college basketball continued to grow. Conferences emerged, especially in the eastern United States, and the rules evolved. Still, the game's following could not match that of college football. The shot clock had not yet been added to college basketball, so teams could hold on to the ball as long as they liked without shooting. To many fans, the action was simply too slow and the scores too low.

THE 1904 OLYMPICS

By the early 1900s, basketball was getting worldwide notice. It was added to the 1904 Olympic Games in St. Louis, Missouri. Olympic officials invited top college teams to compete in a championship tournament. Hiram College, located in Hiram, Ohio, won the Olympic Intercollegiate World Championship.

While the lack of a shot clock contributed to low-scoring games, what really held the game back was the style of play. Players used two hands and kept both feet on the ground while shooting. The shot was easy to defend, and scoring was difficult. This style led to many dull, plodding contests. In 1936, Stanford player Hank Luisetti thrilled fans and annoyed defenders with something that would change the game forever: the one-handed jump shot. Basketball historians agree that Luisetti wasn't the first to attempt such a shot. But he used it so well and with such flair that other players had no choice but to perfect it themselves. Almost overnight, the game changed. It became faster, more focused on scoring, and more thrilling.

Hank Luisetti helped popularize basketball with his exciting style of play.

THE TOURNAMENT ERA BEGINS

The dawn of the jump shot had changed the face of college basketball. But the sport still had one nagging problem. At season's end, fans had conference champions to celebrate, but no real *national* champ. In 1938, the Metropolitan Basketball Writers Association in New York City had a solution. They came up with an invitation-only tournament featuring the best teams in the country to determine, once and for all, who was No. 1. The National Invitation Tournament (NIT) was born. A committee selected six teams to participate in the first NIT, to be held annually at Madison Square Garden in New York City. Temple defeated Colorado, 60–36, to claim the first NIT title.

In 1959, Hank Luisetti *(left)* was enshrined in the Basketball Hall of Fame.

The NCAA was not far behind. The organization had formed in 1906 to reform college football, which at the time had been a brutal and sometimes deadly sport. In the decades since, the NCAA had taken over as a governing body for all major college athletics. In 1939—a year after the NIT had formed—the NCAA introduced a men's basketball tournament of its own. That first NCAA tournament featured eight teams. One

THE FATE OF THE NIT

The NIT remained an important tournament through the end of the 1950s. But as the NCAA tournament field grew and the balance of college basketball power shifted west to teams such as UCLA, the New York–based NIT became an afterthought. By the 1970s, many fans and players joked about the "other" tournament. Some said that NIT really stood for Not Invited Tournament or Nobody's Interested Tournament. However, the NIT is still played each season, giving smaller schools and young, rising teams a chance to taste postseason action.

champion was selected from each of eight regions. After the opening round of games, the first semifinal round was set: Oregon, Oklahoma, Villanova, and Ohio State. Then, in the title game, Oregon beat Ohio State, 46–33, to become the first NCAA champion.

The NCAA had its champion, but which team was best in the country? Though Oregon won the NCAA tournament in 1939, Long Island defeated Loyola to win the NIT. In those early years, the top teams were often invited to both tournaments and had to choose one or the other. The NIT, played in New York City, was often the first choice.

Over the next few years, some teams competed in both tournaments—but rarely with success. In 1940, Colorado won the NIT but lost in the early rounds of the NCAA. Then, in 1944, Utah was the NCAA champ but lost in the opening round of the NIT.

In 1950, City College of New York (CCNY) and Bradley University met in the championship games of both the NIT and the NCAA. City College won both games, becoming the only team to win both tournaments in a single year. They were the first true champions of college basketball. Shortly after, the NCAA ruled that teams could participate in only one postseason tournament. As time went on, the NCAA tournament emerged as the bracket of choice among the nation's top teams. The NIT gradually declined into its modern role as a consolation bracket.

John Wooden *(right)* helped make UCLA a college basketball powerhouse in the 1960s and 1970s.

THE EXPANDING FIELD

With the NIT's importance fading, the NCAA acted quickly to expand its tournament. In 1951, it doubled the field from eight teams to 16. At the time, only conference champions were eligible for the tournament. Yet 16 spots in the tournament still weren't enough to include all the conferences. The field expanded again in 1953, this time to 22 teams. For the next two decades, the size of the field ranged between 22 and 25 teams.

The size of the field wasn't the only thing about the NCAA tournament that was changing. In the early days of college basketball, teams from the East Coast tended to control the tournament. But by the 1960s, the balance of power was shifting west on the broad shoulders of one program: UCLA. Led by legendary coach John Wooden, the UCLA Bruins won their first championship in 1964. They defeated Duke, 98–83, to complete a perfect 30–0 season. It was the start of a winning run of the kind rarely seen in team sports. Over a 12-season stretch from 1964 to 1975, UCLA won the NCAA tournament 10 times. That included a streak of seven titles in a row from 1967 to 1973.

As the UCLA dynasty died with the retirement of Wooden in 1975, a new tournament era was beginning. The NCAA faced growing criticism for allowing only conference champions into the tournament. In 1971, USC of the Pacific-8 (Pac-8)

THE WOMEN'S BRACKET

The early 1980s was a time of rapid expansion in the men's NCAA tournament. But the growth of college basketball postseason play didn't stop there. In 1982, the NCAA hosted its first women's tournament—with a 32-team bracket. Louisiana Tech won that first NCAA title, defeating Cheyney University, 76–62.

Like the men's tournament, the women's grew quickly. By 1994, it matched the men's bracket in size at 64 teams. It has remained at that number since. Aside from UCLA's winning run of the late 1960s and early 1970s, the men's game has had many different champions. The women's tournament, on the other hand, has been marked by a handful of programs that seem to win the title every year. Most notable among them are Tennessee and Connecticut, who combined to win more than half of the women's championships from 1982 to 2015.

Conference finished the season ranked No. 3 in the nation. But because UCLA won the Pac-8, USC was left out of the tournament. Three years later, fourth-ranked Maryland was also left out. The NCAA responded in 1975 by expanding the field to 32 teams. The new rules allowed two teams from each conference to enter the tournament. The larger field attracted a wider audience, and the hype surrounding the tournament's final games grew. *Cleveland Plain Dealer* sportswriter Ed Chay coined the phrase *final four* to describe the last four teams in the tournament that season, and the name stuck. By 1978, the lowercase name had been adopted and capitalized by the NCAA. The Final Four had arrived.

Birth of the Bracket

To modern college basketball fans, filling out an NCAA tournament bracket is a March tradition. From casual fans predicting the outcomes just for fun, to office pools for cash, to big-dollar gambling operations, it seems almost everyone makes their picks. Even the president of the United States gets in on the action. Fans love to discuss their brackets. They brag about upsets correctly picked and complain about bracket-busters (top seeds that have fallen in the early rounds).

This cultural phenomenon started in a Staten Island, New York, bar in 1977. Eighty-eight patrons each paid $10 to fill out a bracket, with the owner of the most accurate bracket taking all the cash. The idea soon spread to offices around the nation—and the world. By 2014, an estimated 60 million Americans filled out at least one bracket, with wagering—both legal and illegal—in the billions of dollars. That same year, billionaire Warren Buffet offered a cool $1 billion to anyone who could correctly predict all 67 tournament games. The odds of such a perfect bracket are beyond long—one in more than nine quintillion. That's a 9 with 18 zeroes behind it!

United States president and basketball fan Barack Obama *(right)* holds up an NCAA bracket in 2010.

THE MODERN FIELD TAKES SHAPE

The late 1970s and early 1980s provided college basketball fans with a string of memorable Final Four games. Fans were wowed by the epic 1979 clash between Earvin "Magic" Johnson's Michigan State Spartans and Larry Bird's Indiana State Sycamores. In 1982, Michael Jordan led the North Carolina Tar Heels to a dramatic championship. The quality of the games, along with improved television broadcasts, made the NCAA tournament one of the biggest events in sports. The tournament, and especially the Final Four, had become wildly popular with fans and raked in money from ticket sales, television deals, and other avenues. The NCAA cashed in further by expanding the field four times over six years, resulting in 64 teams.

The field remained at 64 teams for the next 16 years. Television ratings soared. Even the announcement of each year's tournament bracket became a popular event. The larger field forced teams to play more and more games to reach the Final Four. The tournament stretched out to almost a month, giving

Duke Blue Devils players celebrate after defeating the Wisconsin Badgers for the NCAA national title in 2015.

rise to the term "March Madness." In 2001, the NCAA began to add play-in games. By 2011, the tournament had reached the modern total of 68 teams. Yet through it all—from the thrill of Cinderella teams to breathtaking, game-winning buzzer-beaters—the jewel of the tournament has always remained the Final Four.

2 DOWN TO THE WIRE

The Greatest Games of the Final Four

For more than 75 years, the Final Four has been giving fans measures of excitement, drama, and heartbreak. While some games have been forgettable, others live on in the memories of basketball fans everywhere. From hard-fought nail-biters to stunning upsets to stirring comebacks, here are some of the greatest games in the history of the Final Four.

WORKING OVERTIME

North Carolina vs. Michigan State, 1957
North Carolina vs. Kansas, 1957

The 1957 North Carolina Tar Heels experienced a Final Four unlike any before or since. Perfect in the regular season, the Tar Heels cruised through the early rounds of the NCAA tournament. They carried the nation's top ranking and a spotless 30–0 record into the Final Four, where the stage was set for two of the greatest games in college basketball history.

It started with an epic battle against the Michigan State Spartans that went to overtime. With 11 seconds left in overtime, Michigan State appeared to have the game in hand. They held a two-point lead, with center John Green on the free-throw line. There was no three-point shot in college basketball in 1957. If Green could make his free throw, Michigan State would have a three-point lead and would probably win the game. But Green missed it. North Carolina forward Pete Brennan snatched the rebound and drove the length of the court. Brennan pulled up and drained the tying jumper as time ran out. The game went to a second overtime and then to a third. That's when the Tar Heels finally pulled away with a 74–70 triple-overtime victory.

It was on to the championship game to face second-ranked Kansas and their superstar center, Wilt Chamberlain. The dream matchup between the nation's top two teams more than lived up to expectations—some have called it the greatest championship game ever played. North Carolina coach Frank McGuire knew that Chamberlain was capable of dominating, so he started the game with a ploy to throw off the big man's concentration. McGuire sent his shortest player, 5-foot-11 guard Tommy Kearns, out to face the 7-foot Chamberlain for the opening tip. "Wilt looked 10 feet tall towering over Tommy, but they made such a ridiculous picture that Chamberlain must have felt no bigger than his thumb," McGuire later explained.

Wilt Chamberlain *(holding the ball)* was one of the greatest college basketball players of all time.

At first, the tactic seemed to work. North Carolina built an early 19–7 lead. But Chamberlain couldn't be kept down so easily. He and Kansas chipped away and finally took a second-half lead, 40–37.

In 1957, college basketball had no shot clock. Kansas was free to stall, passing the ball around without really looking for a shot. North Carolina responded by fouling Chamberlain on purpose, as the big man was not a skilled free-throw shooter. The strategy worked, but it was costly. The Tar Heels' best player, Lennie Rosenbluth, fouled out of the game with 1:45 to play. Still, North Carolina managed to hit a free throw in the final seconds to force overtime.

North Carolina players surround Wilt Chamberlain *(with the ball)* in an attempt to keep the game's best player from scoring.

The first overtime was a defensive struggle. Neither team was willing to take any chances, and each made only a single basket. The game remained tied, 48–48. In the second overtime, neither team scored a single point!

The scoring finally picked up in the third overtime. North Carolina jumped ahead with two quick baskets, but Chamberlain powered Kansas back to a 53–52 lead. Time was running out.

North Carolina's Joe Quigg brought the ball up the court with just 10 seconds remaining. Quigg drove toward the basket—right at Chamberlain. After a quick pump fake, Quigg rose up and fired. Chamberlain swatted the ball away, but guard Maurice King fouled Quigg.

With six seconds remaining, Quigg drained both free throws to put North Carolina ahead. Kansas attempted one last desperation play, but Quigg tipped away an errant pass and time ran out. North Carolina had done it! It had taken six overtimes in two days, but their perfect season was complete.

CUTTING DOWN THE NETS

Every sport has its traditional celebrations. Football players douse championship coaches with Gatorade. Winning drivers in auto racing do burnouts or victory laps. In college basketball, the champions bust out a ladder and scissors to cut down the nets.

The tradition dates back to Indiana high school basketball in the 1920s. Everett Case was the head coach of Frankfort, one of the state's dominant teams. Case won four state titles with Frankfort, and after each one, he encouraged his players to take home something to remind them of what they'd accomplished. *Something* quickly became a piece of the net.

Two decades later, while coaching for North Carolina State (NC State), Case brought the tradition to the college ranks. In 1947, NC State celebrated a conference title by cutting down the nets. The gymnasium didn't have any ladders handy, so Case's players hoisted him up to do the job. The tradition caught on, and soon players and coaches around the nation were celebrating conference championships and national titles by taking a little piece of net home with them.

Kiah Stokes of the Connecticut Huskies cuts down the net after helping her team win the women's NCAA tournament in 2015.

WOODEN'S LAST RUN
UCLA vs. Louisville, 1975

Including 32 teams for the first time, the 1975 NCAA tournament marked the beginning of rapid expansion of its bracket. But while change was in the air, one thing remained constant: the domination of John Wooden's UCLA Bruins.

Sharpshooting Louisville looked to bring an end to UCLA dominance in their semifinal tilt with the Bruins. Louisville battled the Bruins to overtime. With 20 seconds to go, Louisville held a 74–73 advantage and had Terry Howard on the free-throw line. Howard had been a perfect 28 for 28 from the stripe that season. Yet when Howard took his first shot of a one-and-one (meaning he'd get a second free throw only if he made the first), he missed.

A UCLA player puts up a shot against Louisville in the 1975 Final Four.

The Bruins grabbed the rebound and quickly called time-out. Wooden drew up a play. With just seconds to go, Marques Johnson flipped a pass to Richard Washington, who rose and fired a jump shot. *Swish!* Just two seconds remained. When Louisville fumbled the inbounds pass, it was over. UCLA was headed back to the championship game.

Yet the surprises didn't end there. After the game, Wooden shocked UCLA fans—and college basketball fans around the nation—by announcing that the 1975 title game would be his last game as a coach. Fittingly, Wooden and the Bruins won the game against Kentucky, 92–85, sending the legendary coach out as a champion. The 1975 Final Four marked yet another high point in an amazing UCLA dynasty, yet it also marked the end. Without Wooden at the helm, UCLA's dominance of college basketball was over.

THE PERFECT GAME
Villanova vs. Georgetown, 1985

In the 1985 NCAA tournament, nobody saw Villanova coming. The Wildcats had endured a largely forgettable season. Among the low points was their final regular-season game, an 85–62 nationally televised drubbing at the hands of Pittsburgh. With a modest 18–9 regular-season record, even a No. 8 seed seemed generous for the Wildcats. Yet against all odds, the Wildcats made one of the most unlikely runs in NCAA tournament history.

It started with a nail-biting two-point victory over ninth-seeded Dayton. The win was hardly a shot of confidence for the Wildcats. But then something clicked. Villanova defeated top-seeded Michigan, fifth-seeded Maryland, second-seeded North Carolina, and second-seeded Memphis State on the way to a shocking appearance in the title game. There, the Wildcats would face their greatest challenge yet, the defending national champion Georgetown Hoyas. Led by superstar center Patrick Ewing, the 1984–1985 Hoyas were considered to be one of the most powerful teams in the history of the sport.

Villanova's Harold Pressley goes up for a basket in the 1985 title game.

The teams, Big East rivals, were quite familiar with each other. Georgetown had beaten the Wildcats in both of their regular-season tilts. Fans really had little reason to expect anything other than another Hoyas victory. Yet it was Villanova taking control of the game early. Center Ed Pinckney, dwarfed by Ewing both in size and raw ability, was a spark for his team. Pinckney battled down low and more than held his own against the game's best big man.

It was a wire-to-wire nail-biter, with neither team able to build much of an advantage. Nursing a slim lead in the final minutes, Villanova employed a smothering zone defense, forcing turnovers and scoring on the other end. It seemed, at times, that the Wildcats couldn't miss. They shot a scorching 79 percent from the field—making 22 of their 28 shots. And down the stretch, when Georgetown was forced to foul to stop the clock, Villanova answered the bell at the free-throw line. They made 22 of 27 free throws in the game—an 82 percent clip. The Hoyas fought furiously in the closing minutes, but the Wildcats held on as the final seconds ticked away, 66–64. It took what many called a perfect game, but Villanova pulled it off—the lowest-seeded team ever to claim the championship.

HOME COOKING
Kansas vs. Oklahoma, 1988

It wasn't quite a home-court advantage for the Kansas Jayhawks when they faced the Oklahoma Sooners in the 1988 title game. But with the game in Kansas City, Missouri—a scant 40 miles from the University of Kansas campus—it felt pretty close.

Despite playing practically in their own backyard, the Jayhawks were heavy underdogs. The Sooners had already beaten Kansas twice that season during conference play. Yet Kansas, unranked at the end of the regular season, had one big thing going its way—superstar forward Danny Manning.

"Let's go play," Manning told his teammates before the game. "Let's have fun. We're not supposed to be here. But we are."

The rivals put on a shooting clinic. The NCAA had added the three-point shot to the sport in 1986–1987. In the first half alone, the two teams made a combined 11 of 16 three-point attempts. The half ended in a 50–50 deadlock—a record for the most combined points in the first half of a title game. But the real fireworks came in the second half. Manning almost singlehandedly kept Kansas in the game. Every time Oklahoma threatened to pull away, Manning was there. He grabbed rebounds and played stout defense while pouring in a game-high 31 points.

Danny Manning *(with the ball)* led his team to victory after victory in the 1988 NCAA tournament.

With 40 seconds to play, Kansas clung to a 78–75 lead. Oklahoma guard Mookie Blaylock drove the ball and knocked down an off-balance, spinning jumper to cut the lead to a single point. A few seconds later, Oklahoma fouled Kansas guard Scooter Barry, who made his first free throw before clanging the second off the rim for a miss. Manning, who had dominated the boards all night, rose up once again. He used his long arms to snatch his 18th rebound of the night and forced the Sooners to foul him. Manning stepped to the line and made both free throws to extend the Kansas lead to four points.

The Sooners were desperate. They raced down the court, and guard Ricky Grace scored on a layup with seven seconds to go. Kansas inbounded the ball to Manning, who was fouled immediately. If he missed either free throw, the sharpshooting Sooners would have a chance. But Manning had carried the Jayhawks so far, and he stepped up again, making both shots to lock down the victory. Danny and the Miracles, as the team was called, cut down the nets to celebrate the Jayhawks' first championship since 1952.

ON THE LINE
Michigan vs. Seton Hall, 1989

Every championship-caliber team deals with some sort of adversity during the course of a season. But few can match what the Michigan Wolverines endured in 1989. The squad, led by sharpshooting guard Glen Rice, put together a solid season, finishing third in the tough Big Ten. Then, before the tournament, news leaked out that head coach Bill Frieder had accepted a job to coach Arizona State the following season. Michigan athletic director Bo Schembechler, a tough-minded former Michigan football coach who was fiercely loyal to the university, wasn't about to let Frieder finish out the season. He fired Frieder on the spot, replacing him with assistant coach Steve Fisher—all just days before the tournament.

And so Fisher took over. In his first game as head coach of Michigan, the No. 3-seeded

Wolverines defeated Xavier in the opening round. It was the start of something big. Whether it was Fisher's coaching or Rice's red-hot shooting, the Wolverines advanced all the way to the final game. There, they faced Seton Hall. The Pirates had already shocked Duke with a comeback from 18 points down to punch their ticket to the title game.

It was a rough, tough, physical affair with plenty of contact in the paint and more than a few flying elbows. Yet, despite the physical play, each team's star—Rice for Michigan and John Morton for Seton Hall—shined. Michigan had the lead at halftime, 37–32.

Seton Hall charged back in the second half with smothering

Seton Hall's Andrew Gaze *(left)* and Michigan's Glen Rice scramble for a loose ball during the final game of the NCAA tournament in 1989.

defense and a flurry of baskets from Morton. With just over a minute to go, the Pirates led, 68–66. Rice put Michigan back in front, rising over a defender to drain a three-pointer. Michigan extended the lead to three points a few moments later.

But Morton had an answer once again, this time knocking down a three-pointer to tie it with just seconds to go. Rice got off a 17-foot jumper as time expired, but it rimmed out. Overtime! It was the first time in 26 years that the title game would go to an extra session.

The Pirates were in control, leading 79–78 with just 10 seconds to go in overtime. Michigan guard Rumeal Robinson charged down the court with the ball. Without hesitation, Robinson drove into the lane. Seton Hall guard Gerald Greene moved to defend. The two made contact, and the referee blew the whistle—a controversial foul on Greene.

Robinson stepped to the stripe with everything on the line. It wasn't a new feeling for him. Earlier in the year, he'd faced a nearly identical situation against Wisconsin—and had missed both shots. Not this time. Robinson calmly swished the first free throw to tie it. The arena was going wild as he set himself up for the second shot. *Swish.* 80–79, Wolverines! Seton Hall's Darryl Walker put up a desperation shot, but it was off the mark. The celebration was on for Fisher and Michigan.

"I think we ought to interview Steve Fisher [for the head coaching position]," joked Schembechler after the game.

Needless to say, Fisher got the job.

Coach Steve Fisher cuts down the net.

UNBEATABLE?

Duke vs. UNLV, 1991

The 1991 University of Nevada, Las Vegas (UNLV) Runnin' Rebels looked, at times, more like an NBA team than a college basketball squad. UNLV, their roster loaded with future pro stars, was riding a 45-game winning streak entering the 1991 Final Four. That streak stretched back to their championship the year before, which had included a 103–73 dismantling of the Duke Blue Devils in the title game.

After cruising through the opening rounds of the 1991 tournament, UNLV seemed unbeatable. As they prepared to face Duke again, this time in the semifinals, the Runnin' Rebels were overwhelming favorites. But UNLV fans, expecting another blowout, were quickly disappointed. The game was close from wire to wire, featuring a stunning 17 ties and 25 lead changes.

The turning point came with 3:51 to play in the game. UNLV held a 74–71 lead, and star point guard Greg Anthony was running the offense. Anthony drove toward the hoop, but he was called for a charging foul. It was his fifth of the game, sending him to the bench for good. UNLV would miss him badly on both ends of the court.

The Runnin' Rebels led 76–71 with just over two minutes to play. That's when Duke point guard Bobby Hurley brought the ball up the court and drained a three-pointer to make the score 76–74. Then the Blue Devils forced a turnover to get the ball back.

With 1:02 to play, Duke's Brian Davis converted a three-point play to give his team the lead. UNLV forward Larry Johnson tied it with a free throw 12 seconds later, 77–77. The crowd was going nuts.

Duke's Tyrone Hill missed on a short jump shot with 15 seconds to go. But Blue Devils forward Christian Laettner was there to collect the rebound, forcing a UNLV foul. With 12.7 seconds to play, Laettner calmly sank both free throws to put Duke up two.

Duke's Christian Laettner
dribbles past a UNLV defender.

UNLV had one last shot. All-American forward Larry Johnson received the inbounds pass. Johnson faked a three-point shot, but Laettner didn't bite on the fake. Johnson was forced to dish the ball to guard Anderson Hunt, who launched a three-point shot. The shot was flat and clanged off the rim. The final seconds ticked away before UNLV had any chance to recover the ball, and the Duke players poured onto the court to celebrate one of the biggest upsets in Final Four history.

CAT FIGHT
Arizona vs. Kentucky, 1997

The 1997 title game featured two schools, Arizona and Kentucky, bearing the same nickname: the Wildcats. Yet aside from the name, the teams had little in common.

Kentucky was the defending champion, built on size, experience, and star power. Arizona, meanwhile, had finished just fifth in its own conference. They were young, inexperienced, and leaned heavily on their outside game.

Knowing that Arizona wanted to launch shots from long distances, Kentucky focused its defense on denying the three-pointer. Arizona took advantage. Time and again, Arizona players passed up long shots to drive the ball toward the hoop.

Bennett Davison *(right)* of the Arizona Wildcats chases down the ball during the 1997 championship game.

"They were coming out so hard [to defend the three-point shot] that the penetration was there all night," said Arizona guard Miles Simon, who scored a game-high 30 points.

Kentucky, slow to adjust to Arizona's new strategy, quickly found itself in foul trouble. Four Kentucky Wildcats would eventually foul out of the game. Among those in foul trouble was star guard Ron Mercer, who was forced to the bench for long stretches of the game.

And yet, despite everything, Kentucky was a team loaded with talent. Arizona simply could not put them away. With about a minute to play in the game, Arizona led, 72–68. That's when Mercer drained a basket from long range. Arizona answered by converting a layup, but then Anthony Epps drilled another three-pointer to tie it, 74–74. It was on to overtime.

Arizona kept the pressure on in overtime, driving to the lane again and again. They went to the free-throw line 14 times in the overtime session, converting on 10 of those shots. Arizona closed out the defending champs without making a single shot from the field in overtime.

After the final seconds of an 84–79 Arizona victory ticked away, Simon collapsed under the basket, clutching the ball and weeping in happiness and disbelief. His head coach, Lute Olson, seemed to have a similar feeling. "I still have a hard time believing this has really happened," Olson confessed after the game.

Arizona's A. J. Bramlett holds a newspaper with the headline ARIZONA WINS after his team beat Kentucky in the 1997 title game.

NOT AGAIN!

Duke and Maryland just couldn't get away from each other in 2001. The conference rivals split a pair of regular-season tilts. Then Duke bounced Maryland out of the Atlantic Coast Conference Tournament. After that game, Duke forward Shane Battier told Maryland guard Juan Dixon, "See you in Minneapolis."

Battier's prediction that the teams would meet in a rare fourth matchup in Minneapolis, Minnesota—the site of the 2001 Final Four—came true. The stakes were higher than ever this time, with the winner earning the right to face Arizona in the championship game.

Shane Battier of Duke *(with the ball)* is surrounded by Maryland defenders during the 2001 Final Four.

Duke had staged huge comebacks in each of its two previous wins over Maryland. In their first game, the Blue Devils had charged from 10 down with less than a minute to play to win in overtime. So Maryland fans couldn't have felt comfortable even as they watched their Terrapins charge out to a huge first-half advantage. They led, 39–17, just over 12 minutes into the game.

As helpless as Duke appeared in those opening minutes, everything changed when head coach Mike Krzyzewski called time-out and ordered his Blue Devils to focus. The players responded, and Duke trimmed the lead to 11 points by halftime. In the second half, the Duke defense clamped down on Dixon, while the Blue Devils knocked down 53 percent of their shots from the

Duke's Jason Williams brings the ball up the floor.

field. Jason Williams drilled a three-pointer with less than seven minutes remaining to complete the frantic comeback and to give Duke its first lead, 73–72.

Maryland, watching Duke wipe out a large deficit for the third time that season, never recovered. Duke cruised the rest of the way. They won, 95–84, and punched their ticket to the championship game (which they won). The 22-point comeback remains the largest in the history of the Final Four.

CRUNCH TIME
Connecticut vs. Duke, 2004

It was a big-time clash between big-time teams when Duke and Connecticut (UConn) met in the 2004 NCAA semifinals. Yet early on, this battle between two of college basketball's most successful programs looked like a yawner. Duke took control early by focusing its defense on Connecticut center Emeka Okafor. The big All-American didn't score a single point in the first half. On the other end of the floor, Okafor was plagued with foul trouble and forced to sit long stretches on the bench.

Without their superstar to lead the way, the Huskies seemed outmatched by the Blue Devils. Duke controlled the action from the opening tap. With less than four minutes to play, they held a seemingly comfortable 75–67 lead.

"It's easy to . . . see yourself down by eight with like next to nothing on the clock . . . and just give up," Okafor said. "It's hard to believe you can do it and put the effort to actually make it happen."

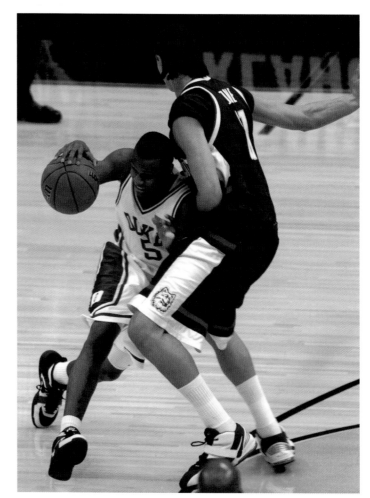

Duke player Daniel Ewing *(left)* dribbles around UConn's Josh Boone.

Connecticut players celebrate their victory over Duke.

But that's just what UConn did. Rashad Anderson drained a three-pointer to cut the lead to five points. Ben Gordon trimmed it to three with a pair of free throws. Then Okafor took over. With a series of fakes, ducks, and spins, the big man knocked down two straight baskets to put the Huskies ahead, 76–75.

With 26 seconds to go, Duke put the ball into the hands of guard J. J. Redick. Redick wasted little time driving to the hoop, looking for either a basket or a foul call. He didn't get either. Anderson and Okafor stripped the ball free. Anderson tracked down the loose ball and was quickly fouled. He made both shots, leaving Duke with only a desperation three-point attempt that clanged off the iron. Despite being outplayed for most of the game, the Huskies had pulled off the comeback to stun the Blue Devils. They advanced to the final, where they defeated Georgia Tech to claim the championship.

DEKKER'S DAGGERS
Wisconsin vs. Kentucky, 2015

In 2015, the Kentucky Wildcats were on a quest to become college basketball's first unbeaten team in nearly four decades. Their roster, stocked with blue-chip recruits and future NBA draft picks, cruised to a perfect regular season. Their spotless record stood at 38–0 entering the Final Four.

That's when they ran into Wisconsin. The Badgers, despite being a fellow No. 1 seed, were heavy underdogs. They didn't boast the star players and perfect record that Kentucky brought to the game. Wisconsin used experience and a finely tuned system designed by head coach Bo Ryan to make up for the apparent talent gap between the teams. As the game dragged on, the Wildcats were unable to pull away.

Kentucky clung to a 60–56 lead with about 4:30 to play. That's when Wisconsin forward Sam Dekker stepped up. Dekker nailed a jump shot to cut the lead in half. Dekker struck again with the game tied at 60. He dribbled, stepped back beyond the three-point arc, and launched. *Swish!* 63–60, Badgers!

Dekker wasn't done. On the other end, Kentucky's Trey Lyles drove toward the hoop with just over a minute to play. Dekker got to the spot first and drew a charging foul on Lyles. The Badgers' forward made one of his two free throws.

Sam Dekker of the Wisconsin Badgers looks to pass the ball.

The Wildcats couldn't stop Wisconsin's offensive attack.

Kentucky's furious comeback attempt fell short, their bid for perfection was dashed, and the celebration was on for the Badgers. It was one of the biggest Final Four upsets in recent memory, but the Badgers were unable to carry that momentum into the title game, where they lost to Duke.

3 UNFORGETTABLE
Memorable Moments of the Final Four

It's not just epic clashes that get college basketball fans excited about the Final Four. Sometimes it's a wild play, a historic occasion, an inspired performance, or a desperation shot that has people talking. Although not all of these games were classics, each provided a moment that fans of the Final Four will never forget.

PRYOR'S MIRACLE
Oklahoma vs. Texas, 1947

The 1947 Final Four saw a classic border battle between Texas and Oklahoma. Texas, which had already beaten Oklahoma during the regular season, held a 54–53 lead in the final seconds of their semifinal game. Oklahoma needed a miracle. Little-used backup Ken Pryor—who hadn't yet recorded a single point in the game—launched a desperation shot from half-court. The ball banked off the backboard and rattled through the net. Stunned, Texas was unable to respond in what little time remained, and Oklahoma walked off with a victory for the ages. To add insult to injury, the two teams shared a train after the game, forcing the Texas players to relive the defeat as the Oklahoma celebration rolled on.

BRADLEY'S UNLIKELY RUN
Bradley vs. USC, 1954

The 1954 NCAA tournament was anything but ordinary. Kentucky, at 25–0, seemed like an obvious favorite to win it all. But the Wildcats suffered a major blow when three of their players were ruled ineligible for the tournament based on a rule about fifth-year players. Rather than show up with a partial roster, the Wildcats declined the tournament invitation altogether.

Meanwhile, the unranked Bradley Braves had scuffled to an unimpressive 15–12 regular-season mark. But Bradley was able to string together tournament upsets of Oklahoma City, Colorado, and Oklahoma State to punch its ticket to the Final Four. The Braves had become one of the tournament's first Cinderella teams.

That's when Bradley ran into USC. The Braves' magical run seemed to be over when they fell behind by seven points late in the fourth quarter. Big comebacks aren't at all uncommon in the modern era. But in 1954, with no shot clock and no three-point line, overcoming such a large margin was a much taller order.

In the 1950s, college basketball games were often low-scoring affairs.

Yet Bradley had one more surprise left. Guard Bob Carney led a frantic last-minute charge, scoring five points in the final 1:05 of play to give the Braves another upset, 74–72. The Braves had earned an unlikely trip to the title game. The magic ended there, with a loss to La Salle in the first nationally televised championship game. But Carney's heroics and Bradley's unlikely run set a standard by which future Cinderella teams could be measured.

A NEW ERA
Texas Western vs. Kentucky, 1966

The 1960s were a time of radical social change in the United States. Minorities were embroiled in a long, bitter struggle for civil rights. A century after the end of slavery in the United States, blacks were still denied equal access and equal opportunities.

That was just as true on the basketball court as in the wider world. In 1966, some major colleges remained segregated—they allowed white students only. Even among integrated teams, there was a feeling among many fans and coaches that a team of all black players would have no chance to succeed.

Texas Western—the school later changed its name to the University of Texas at El Paso (UTEP)—head coach Don Haskins felt differently. In that 1965–1966 season, Haskins made the Texas Western Miners the first major college program ever to start five black players in a game. And they were good. The Miners lost just one game all season and advanced to the title game. There, they faced the top-ranked team in the country, Kentucky. The Wildcats were a member of the still-segregated Southeastern Conference.

It was a true clash of styles and ideas. Ten players stepped onto the court for the opening tip. All five Kentucky players were white. All five Texas Western players were black.

Leading up to the game, many reporters suggested that Texas Western would have no chance and that their style lacked the discipline needed to beat a team as good as

Kentucky. Even Kentucky head coach Adolph Rupp vowed before the game that five black players would never beat his Wildcats.

Texas Western proved that they were every bit as good as Kentucky. "We played the most intelligent, the most boring, the most disciplined game of them all," said Miners guard Willie Worsley.

The game itself may have been unspectacular. But the result—a 72–65 Miners victory—would help change the sport forever. Within five years, racial segregation in college sports was all but over.

Kentucky's Larry Conley takes a shot against Texas Western.

A Cold Reception

Texas Western faced hostility on every front during their 1966 title run. Fans in the stands waved Confederate flags—symbols of slavery and racial prejudice—during their games. The bigotry continued even after the title game. It was traditional for the winning team to cut down the nets in celebration. But no one in the arena would bring the Miners a ladder. Other players had to hoist Willie Worsley onto their shoulders to cut the nets.

The insults kept coming after the nets were down. The NCAA basketball champions were traditionally invited to appear on the popular TV program *The Ed Sullivan Show*. But no such invitation ever came to Texas Western. Kentucky coach Rupp claimed that the Miners had cheated and that the black players weren't real students. For years, Rupp refused to let it go. It would be three more seasons before Kentucky welcomed its first black player. The Southeastern Conference, of which Kentucky was a member, didn't fully integrate until 1972. Even then, black players often faced threats and abuse from fans.

WHO'S NO. 1?
UCLA vs. Houston, 1968

The 1967–1968 Houston Cougars seemed completely unstoppable. Even the powerful UCLA Bruins had been helpless to slow down the Cougars and national player of the year Elvin Hayes during the regular season. So when No. 1-ranked Houston drew a rematch with No. 2-ranked UCLA in the semifinals, few fans expected a different result.

The fans couldn't have been more wrong. Legendary UCLA coach John Wooden had learned from his team's earlier loss to Houston. Wooden crafted his entire defense around stopping Hayes, forcing the other, less-talented Houston players to try to step up. It worked. Hayes struggled, scoring only 10 points in the game.

Meanwhile, the Bruins poured it on behind a 19-point, 18-rebound performance by center Lew Alcindor (who later changed his name to Kareem Abdul-Jabbar). UCLA crushed the nation's top team, building a lead as large as 44 points before Wooden pulled his starters and allowed his bench players to get some action. The result was a stunning 101–69 victory.

While the upset itself wasn't that surprising, no one could have predicted that the nation's top-ranked team could be so utterly dominated. Houston coach Guy Lewis called it "the greatest exhibition of basketball I've ever seen." Wooden and the Bruins went on to beat North Carolina to claim the championship and stake their claim as perhaps the greatest team in college basketball history.

THE STREAK ENDS
UCLA vs. North Carolina State, 1974

UCLA's dominance of the NCAA tournament in the late 1960s and early 1970s was stunning. The Bruins entered the 1974 tournament

Lew Alcindor grabs a rebound against Houston in 1968.

seeking their eighth straight championship. By the time they reached the title game, they had a 38-game tournament winning streak.

Their opponent, the NC State Wolfpack, knew that ending such a streak wouldn't be easy. Early on, the Wolfpack appeared well on their way to becoming another footnote in the legend of Wooden and UCLA. The Bruins, behind a stellar effort from center Bill Walton, built an 11-point second-half lead. But star player David Thompson led a frantic NC State charge back to force overtime . . . and then double overtime.

NC State players and fans celebrate the team's victory over UCLA.

UCLA took charge again in double overtime. They led by seven points before the Wolfpack started another charge. Thompson scored a pair of baskets late to put NC State ahead, 78–75, and they held on for the win. The UCLA dynasty wasn't over, but for one year at least, the Bruins had to watch other teams play the championship game. NC State defeated Marquette to claim the title.

END TO END
Marquette vs. UNC Charlotte, 1977

Marquette and University of North Carolina at Charlotte (UNC Charlotte) were knotted at 49 near the end of their 1977 semifinal game. Marquette had possession, but they had to inbound the ball from under their own basket with just three seconds to go. It looked like overtime.

Marquette's Butch Lee got the ball and heaved a pass the length of the court. The ball tipped off a UNC Charlotte player and into the hands of Jerome Whitehead. Whitehead spun, lunged toward the basket, and bounced it through just as time expired. Marquette swarmed the court to celebrate the amazing victory, and the party continued two nights later when they won the national title in head coach Al McGuire's final game.

Many fans of the NCAA tournament are familiar with a similar famous play that happened 15 years later in the regional semifinals. Duke's Grant Hill tossed a court-length pass to Christian Laettner for a last-second, game-winning basket in what some people call the greatest tournament game of all time. But Lee's pass came first, and it came on a bigger stage: the Final Four.

MAGIC VS. BIRD
Michigan State vs. Indiana State, 1979

Many factors have helped the Final Four become the gigantic event it is today, from improved television broadcasts to the expansion of the tournament field. But on the court, no game contributed to the popularity of the Final Four more than the 1979 title match.

The game featured Michigan State vs. Indiana State. But to basketball fans nationwide, the *real* matchup was Magic vs. Bird: Michigan State guard Earvin "Magic" Johnson vs. Indiana State forward Larry Bird.

It was a matchup for the ages. College basketball had enjoyed its share of rising stars over the decades, but rarely had two such talented athletes been at the top at the same time. The chance to see them square off for the title was a dream for the NCAA. The tournament had already begun to grow in

Magic Johnson dunks the ball during the 1979 national championship game.

popularity, but a game had never been so widely anticipated by fans nationwide. Johnson and Bird were a contrast in style. Johnson, from big-time national power Michigan State, was flashy and always willing to speak out. Bird, out of little-known Indiana State, was quiet and reserved. He preferred to let his stellar play do the talking.

The game ultimately failed to deliver on the hype. The result was less about Johnson and Bird and more that Michigan State had a much deeper and talented roster. The Spartans cruised to a 75–64 victory. The lingering image for many was of Bird, towel draped over his head, sobbing in anguish over the only loss of his senior season.

Johnson and Bird would go on to superstardom in the NBA and are credited with igniting greater fan interest in pro basketball. But it all started on a March night in 1979 with Johnson and the Spartans hoisting the trophy.

A STAR IS BORN
North Carolina vs. Georgetown, 1982

Michael Jordan won six NBA titles and is widely regarded as the greatest basketball player of all time. And while Jordan was heavily recruited coming out of high school, no one could have imagined what he would be capable of on a basketball court. He enjoyed a solid yet not overly spectacular freshman season, helping the Tar Heels advance to the 1982 title game.

It was there, on the biggest stage in college basketball, that the legend of Michael Jordan really began. North Carolina faced powerful Georgetown for the title. The game was a nail-biter, with neither team able to build a lead of more than a few points.

Georgetown clung to a 62–61 lead as the clock ticked down to under 20 seconds. North Carolina whipped the ball around the perimeter, keeping the Georgetown defense on the move. Finally, the ball made its way to Jordan on the left wing. The 19-year-old didn't hesitate. He rose up and fired. *Swish!* The basket came with just 15 seconds to play and proved to be the game-winner.

> *"I didn't see it go in. I was just praying it would go. I never did look at the ball."*
> —Michael Jordan, on his 1982 game-winning shot

Michael Jordan puts up the game-winning shot.

TIME-OUT? GAME OVER
Michigan vs. North Carolina, 1993

The Michigan Wolverines, led by five freshmen known as the Fab Five, had advanced to the 1992 title game before falling to Duke. The next year, as sophomores, the Fab Five were looking to win it all. After a thrilling overtime victory over Kentucky in the semifinal, only the North Carolina Tar Heels stood in Michigan's way.

The title game was a hard-fought, back-and-forth struggle. With 46 seconds to play in the game, Michigan's Ray Jackson drained a jumper to pull the Wolverines within three points, 72–69. Michigan immediately called time-out—its final time-out of the half—to set up its defense. They quickly forced a North Carolina turnover, and guard Jalen Rose fired a jumper that clanged off the rim. But superstar forward Chris Webber snagged the rebound, sliced

Chris Webber *(left)* blocks a shot by UNC's Eric Montross.

to the rim, and trimmed the Tar Heels' lead to a single point.

A quick foul on the other end sent UNC's Pat Sullivan to the free-throw line. Sullivan made his first shot but missed the second. Webber snagged the rebound. The big man looked to pass, but his teammates were already headed up the court.

Twenty seconds remained. The crowd was in a frenzy, filling the arena with thunderous cheers. Webber sprinted up the court with the ball. His frantic pace suggested that Webber thought there was less time on the clock than there actually was. North Carolina defenders collapsed around the forward, trapping him.

Strangely, none of Webber's teammates rushed to help him. Seeing the defense bearing down on him, Webber stopped dribbling, leaving himself no escape without a teammate to pass to. With the crowd roaring and the clock ticking, Webber panicked. He lifted his hands and formed a T—the signal for a time-out that Michigan did not have.

Webber's mistake was a technical foul, giving North Carolina two free throws *and* possession of the ball. Any chance Michigan had was dead.

Shocked and visibly shaken, with tears streaming down his face, Webber could only watch as North Carolina celebrated the championship. It would be the final play of Webber's brilliant college career and a moment that few who saw it could ever forget.

Chris Webber looks on in dismay as his team loses to North Carolina.

THE SHOT
Kansas vs. Memphis, 2008

The Memphis Tigers appeared to have their first NCAA basketball championship in their grasp. They led the Kansas Jayhawks by nine with just over two minutes to play in the 2008 title game. But Memphis struggled from the free-throw line in the final minutes, missing four of five shots, to keep the door open for a desperate Jayhawks team.

With 10.8 seconds to go, Kansas trailed by three points. Jayhawks guard Sherron Collins darted down the court, weaving through the Memphis defense. Collins dished the ball to fellow guard Mario Chalmers, who rose up from a foot behind the three-point line to launch a long, desperate shot. *Swish!* The crowd went wild, as did the Kansas bench. Memphis could only look on in disbelief.

"It will probably be the biggest shot ever made in Kansas history," said Kansas coach Bill Self.

Chalmers' shot sent the game to overtime, and it seemed to both ignite Kansas and let the air out of the Tigers. Kansas rolled in the extra session to win, 75–68.

Mario Chalmers elevates for a three-pointer.

SO CLOSE
Duke vs. Butler, 2010

Few people who filled out their 2010 tournament brackets had the Butler Bulldogs—representing a school of just 4,200 students—going far, much less winning it all. And yet the fifth-seeded Bulldogs became one of the greatest Cinderella stories in tournament history by advancing all the way to the title game, where they faced powerhouse Duke.

With just 3.6 seconds to play, Duke led 60–59, with center Brian Zoubek on the free-throw line. Zoubek connected on his first free throw to push the lead to two points. Zoubek

Duke's Brian Zoubek *(No. 55)* stretches for the ball.

had one more free throw coming. That left him with two options. He could try to make the free throw, which would extend the lead to three. Or he could miss it on purpose, forcing Butler—which was out of time outs—to rebound the ball and go the length of the floor in just three seconds. Zoubek and the Blue Devils chose to miss the free throw, which clanged off the rim.

Butler's Gordon Hayward snatched the rebound and raced down the court. Two seconds . . . one second . . . From half-court, Hayward leaped, launching the ball toward the hoop. A crowd of 70,000—most of them backing the underdog Bulldogs—watched as the shot arced toward the hoop. The ball banked off the backboard, onto the rim, and bounced out. It was over, and Duke rushed the court to celebrate yet another national title.

Later, an analysis by ESPN estimated that Hayward missed the shot—and the ultimate storybook ending—by a mere three inches.

Gordon Hayward's half-court shot almost sent Butler to victory.

8 + 11 = 19
BUTLER VS. VIRGINIA COMMONWEALTH, 2011

Final Fours are typically stocked with No. 1 and No. 2 seeds. Yet the 2011 Final Four didn't include any—the first time that has ever happened. Still, the first semifinal, featuring usual powerhouses Connecticut and Kentucky, wasn't shocking to anyone. It was the other semifinal that proved Cinderella was alive and well and could dance all the way to the title game.

Butler, an eight seed, had shocked the basketball world by reaching the Final Four for a second straight season. They faced off against No. 11-seeded Virginia Commonwealth University (VCU) in what is easily the most unlikely Final Four pairing in history. The game itself was forgettable (Butler won, then lost in the title game to Connecticut). But the notion that teams with a combined seeding of *19* could square off on college basketball's biggest stage proved that, in an era of big-time conferences and powerhouse programs, two little-known schools could still battle for a shot at basketball immortality.

NCAA Tournament Champions

YEAR	WINNER	RUNNER-UP
2015	Duke	Wisconsin
2014	Connecticut	Kentucky
2013	Louisville	Michigan
2012	Kentucky	Kansas
2011	Connecticut	Butler
2010	Duke	Butler
2009	North Carolina	Michigan State
2008	Kansas	Memphis
2007	Florida	Ohio State
2006	Florida	UCLA
2005	North Carolina	Illinois
2004	Connecticut	Georgia Tech
2003	Syracuse	Kansas
2002	Maryland	Indiana
2001	Duke	Arizona
2000	Michigan State	Florida
1999	Connecticut	Duke
1998	Kentucky	Utah
1997	Arizona	Kentucky
1996	Kentucky	Syracuse
1995	UCLA	Arkansas
1994	Arkansas	Duke
1993	North Carolina	Michigan
1992	Duke	Michigan
1991	Duke	Kansas
1990	UNLV	Duke
1989	Michigan	Seton Hall
1988	Kansas	Oklahoma
1987	Indiana	Syracuse
1986	Louisville	Duke
1985	Villanova	Georgetown
1984	Georgetown	Houston
1983	North Carolina State	Houston
1982	North Carolina	Georgetown
1981	Indiana	North Carolina
1980	Louisville	UCLA
1979	Michigan State	Indiana State

1978	Kentucky	Duke
1977	Marquette	North Carolina
1976	Indiana	Michigan
1975	UCLA	Kentucky
1974	North Carolina State	Marquette
1973	UCLA	Memphis State
1972	UCLA	Florida State
1971	UCLA	Villanova
1970	UCLA	Jacksonville
1969	UCLA	Purdue
1968	UCLA	North Carolina
1967	UCLA	Dayton
1966	UTEP	Kentucky
1965	UCLA	Michigan
1964	UCLA	Duke
1963	Loyola (IL)	Cincinnati
1962	Cincinnati	Ohio State
1961	Cincinnati	Ohio State
1960	Ohio State	California
1959	California	West Virginia
1958	Kentucky	Seattle
1957	North Carolina	Kansas
1956	San Francisco	Iowa
1955	San Francisco	La Salle
1954	La Salle	Bradley
1953	Indiana	Kansas
1952	Kansas	St. John's
1951	Kentucky	Kansas State
1950	CCNY	Bradley
1949	Kentucky	Oklahoma A&M
1948	Kentucky	Baylor
1947	Holy Cross	Oklahoma
1946	Oklahoma State	North Carolina
1945	Oklahoma State	NYU
1944	Utah	Dartmouth
1943	Wyoming	Georgetown
1942	Stanford	Dartmouth
1941	Wisconsin	Washington State
1940	Indiana	Kansas
1939	Oregon	Ohio State

4 LOOKING AHEAD
The Future of
the Final Four

The modern college game would be all but unrecognizable to that handful of players in the basement of Hamline University's science building more than a century ago. From rim-rattling dunks and knee-buckling crossover dribbles to perfectly arcing three-point shots, the sport has come a long way since the intercollegiate game was born that February day in 1895. And yet after all this time, the college game continues to evolve. Even as its popularity soars, college basketball's long-term future remains very much in flux.

ONE AND DONE

For decades, the college basketball model was built on the idea that student-athletes would play for four seasons, barring injury. Part of a coach's job was to build the proper mix of newcomers and upperclassmen to field a competitive team each year. That began to change in 1969, when Spencer Haywood left college early to sign with the American Basketball Association's Denver Rockets. Haywood's decision eventually led to a Supreme Court ruling that shot down the NBA's requirement that players be four years removed from high school.

For the next several decades, many of the top players followed suit, leaving college early—typically after their junior seasons—to join the pro ranks. But in 1995, when high school star Kevin Garnett declared that he would skip college altogether and enter the NBA Draft, the landscape changed for good. The Minnesota Timberwolves selected Garnett with the fifth pick in that year's draft, and the forward went on to a superstar career. A year later, high school star Kobe Bryant did the same, eventually landing with the Los Angeles Lakers.

Spencer Haywood

The floodgates were open for high school players. For every success story—Garnett, Bryant, LeBron James—there were many more flameouts. It was a situation that neither the NBA nor the NCAA liked. So in 2005, the NBA passed a rule requiring all players to be at least 19 years old and at least one year removed from high school.

The rule set up a new path for would-be NBA players. Suddenly, the nation's top high school players were all but forced to attend college, even though many of them never intended to stay longer than one year before jumping to the NBA. The era of the one-and-done player had begun.

College coaches scrambled to adjust to the new model. In time, many coaches came to embrace the system. Most famously, John Calipari of Kentucky built a program around recruiting likely one-and-done players. He argued that every player he sent to the NBA made his program that much more attractive to future recruits.

While Calipari and others may have embraced the system, its impact on college basketball's fan base is still hard to gauge. Will fans' loyalty—and interest—wane as star players leave for the NBA as quickly as they came? And can the college game itself survive when it lacks consistent star power? Only time will tell.

John Calipari has coached some of college basketball's most successful teams in recent years.

PLAYER COMPENSATION

The first college basketball players were ordinary students, playing the game just for the fun of it. In time, as universities noticed that having a winning team provided a financial benefit to the university, they started to offer scholarships to attract the top players. In 1952, the NCAA formally legalized the practice.

Duke fans cheer during the 2015 Final Four.

Determined that college athletics should remain strictly amateur, the NCAA began to pass and enforce rules ensuring that universities did not pay players to play for their schools. But this created a slippery slope. College coaches found a wealth of ways to skirt the rules—all in the name of winning. Some used university boosters (wealthy fans) to pay players. Some created academic programs that allowed players to graduate without doing much schoolwork. Under-the-table deals threatened the competitive balance of the game, and the NCAA responded by passing rules that were increasingly complex and restrictive.

Meanwhile, the business of college basketball was booming. Only college football made more money for top universities. From ticket sales to billion-dollar TV deals, universities raked in the cash, and coaches began to command salaries in the millions. Many players, fans, and media began to see the structure as unfair. Why should others profit so richly when the athletes themselves were denied any piece of the bounty?

Supporters of the system argued that players were rewarded with a cost-free college education—no small thing—and that no one was forcing them to sign on.

The long-debated issue of pay-for-play jumped into the headlines in 2014 in two major cases. Ed O'Bannon, a former UCLA basketball standout, sued the NCAA on behalf of a group of players. O'Bannon challenged the NCAA's practice of profiting from the images of its players while refusing to allow those same players to market and profit from their own images. In August, US District Court judge Claudia Wilken handed down a decision that agreed, at least in part, with O'Bannon's claim. Wilken ruled, among other things, that universities could hold a portion of profits gained from the use of players' images in a trust, to be distributed to those players upon the completion of their collegiate careers. Wilken's ruling did not require universities to take this step but rather offered them the option of paying players in such a manner.

The O'Bannon case was a landmark, but its ultimate importance may be dwarfed by the actions of the 2014 Northwestern University football team. That year, Northwestern players voted to form a labor union. In doing so, they essentially declared themselves to be not just students of the university but employees as well. As an organized union, the Northwestern players would have more power to negotiate with the university on issues such as money and the treatment of injured players.

Ed O'Bannon played for UCLA from 1991 to 1995.

"We're one step closer to a world where college athletes are not stuck with sports-related medical bills, do not lose their scholarships when they are injured, are not subject to unnecessary brain trauma, and are given better opportunities to complete their degree," said former Northwestern quarterback Kain Colter after the vote. In 2015, the National Labor Relations Board ruled that the players could not form a union. Still, the Northwestern vote brought the idea of paying players to the forefront in college athletics.

College basketball has many challenges ahead. Yet the sport has thrived, and most fans expect that it will continue to do so. The game's rules will change and evolve, its players and coaches will come and go, and the very structure of the NCAA tournament itself may change. But one thing is all but certain to remain constant: the thrill and drama of the Final Four.

Duke and Michigan State clash during the 2015 Final Four.

SOURCE NOTES

17   Barry Wilner and Ken Rappoport, *The Big Dance: The Story of the NCAA Basketball Tournament* (Lanham, MD: Taylor, 2012), 12.

23   Berry Tramel, "1988 NCAA Championship Game: Kansas Played Oklahoma's Game and Lived to Tell about It," *Oklahoman*, April 8, 2013, http://newsok.com/1988-ncaa-championship-game-kansas-played-oklahomas-game-and-lived-to-tell-about-it/article/3780782/?page=2.

26   Robyn Norwood, "NCAA Basketball Championship: Michigan vs. Seton Hall: Wolverines Deck the Hall—Barely: Robinson Hits 2 Free Throws in OT for Win," *Los Angeles Times,* April 4, 1989, http://articles.latimes.com/1989-04-04/sports/sp-1038_1_seton-hall.

29   Malcolm Moran, "Arizona's First Title Denies Kentucky a Repeat," *New York Times,* April 1, 1997, http://www.nytimes.com/1997/04/01/sports/arizona-s-first-title-denies-kentucky-a-repeat.html.

29   Anthony Cotton, "Arizona Wins Cat Fight in Overtime," *Washington Post,* April 1, 1997, http://www.washingtonpost.com/wp-srv/sports/longterm/memories/final4/articles/final97.htm.

30   Hermann Wendorff, "Duke, Maryland Stage Set," *Fayetteville Observer,* January 17, 2002, http://www.fayobserver.com/sports/duke-maryland-stage-set/article_37d9b0bd-f3ec-5678-a822-3c061ab6dd22.html.

32   "Connecticut vs. Duke," *USA Today,* April 3, 2004, http://usatoday30.usatoday.com/sports/scores104/104094/20040403NCAABDUKE------0.htm.

39   Frank Fitzpatrick, "Texas Western's 1966 Title Left Lasting Legacy," *ESPN.com,* November 19, 2003, https://espn.go.com/classic/s/013101_texas_western_fitzpatrick.html.

41   Seth Davis, *Wooden: A Coach's Life* (New York: Times Books, 2014), 305.

44   Greg Logan, "The Top Four Final Four Games," *Newsday,* March 31, 2012, http://www.newsday.com/sports/college/college-basketball/the-top-four-final-four-games-1.3635919

48   Pat Forde, "Chalmers, Kansas Get One Shining Moment," *ESPN.com,* April 8, 2008, http://sports.espn.go.com/espn/columns/story?columnist=forde_pat&id=3335476&sportCat=ncb.

59   "NU Players Cast Secret Ballots," *ESPN.com,* April 26, 2014, http://espn.go.com/chicago/college-football/story/_/id/10837584/northwestern-wildcats-players-vote-whether-form-first-union-college-athletes.

GLOSSARY

buzzer-beater: a last-second basket that wins a game

Cinderella team: a team that advances farther than expected in the NCAA tournament

consolation: a secondary contest or award

dynasty: a period of dominance by one team over at least several seasons

favorite: a team expected to win a game

seed: a ranking for teams entering the tournament that is used to pit the strongest teams against the weakest. Seeds are determined by teams' records, the strength of their opponents, and other factors.

underdog: a team expected to lose a game

upset: a game in which an underdog wins

zone defense: a type of defense where each member of the team defends an area of the court rather than a specific opponent

FURTHER READING

Books

Bekkering, Annalise. *NCAA Basketball.* New York: AV2 by Weigl, 2014.

Berman, Len. *The Greatest Moments in Sports: Upsets and Underdogs.* Naperville, IL: Sourcebooks Jabberwocky, 2012.

Campbell, Forest G., and Fred Ramen. *An Insider's Guide to Basketball.* New York: Rosen Central, 2015.

Cohen, Zachary. *Sports Illustrated Kids Slam Dunk: The Top 10 of Everything in Basketball.* New York: Time Home Entertainment, Inc., 2014

Coy, John. *Game Changer: John McLendon and the Secret Game.* Minneapolis: Carolrhoda Books, 2015.

Gitlin, Marty. *Playing Pro Basketball.* Minneapolis: Lerner Publications, 2015.

Savage, Jeff. *Super Basketball Infographics.* Minneapolis: Lerner Publications, 2015.

Websites

ESPN—College Basketball http://espn.go.com/ncb/
Visit ESPN's college basketball page for scores, schedules, and much more.

NCAA Men's Basketball http://www.ncaa.com/sports/basketball-men
This is the official NCAA men's basketball website. It's the place to explore everything there is to learn about men's college basketball.

NCAA Women's Basketball http://www.ncaa.com/sports/basketball-women
The official website of women's college basketball has enough brackets, rankings, and stories to keep fans satisfied all year.

Sports Reference—College Football http://www.sports-reference.com/cbb
Search through Sports Reference's huge database of college basketball statistics.

INDEX

ABOUT THE AUTHOR

Matt Doeden began his career as a sportswriter, covering everything from high school sports to the NFL. Since then he has written hundreds of children's and young adult books on topics ranging from history to sports to current events. His titles *Sandy Koufax, Tom Brady: Unlikely Champion, The College Football Championship: The Fight for the Top Spot,* and *The World Series: Baseball's Biggest Stage* were Junior Library Guild selections. His title *Darkness Everywhere: The Assassination of Mohandas Gandhi* was listed among the Best Children's Books of the Year by the Children's Book Committee at Bank Street College. Doeden, an avid basketball fan, lives in Minnesota with his wife and two children.

PHOTO ACKNOWLEDGMENTS